MARKS&
SPENCER

pasta
sauces

simple and delicious easy-to-make recipes

Christine McFadden

Marks and Spencer p.l.c.
Baker Street, London, W1U 8EP

www.marksandspencer.com

ISBN: 1-84273-006-1

Printed in Spain

Produced by The Bridgewater Book Company Ltd

BOOK
Photographer Simon Punter
Home Economist Ricky Turner

COVER
Photographer Ian Parsons
Home Economist Sara Hesketh

NOTES FOR THE READER

- This book uses both metric and imperial measurements. Follow the same units of measurement throughout; do not mix metric and imperial.
- All spoon measurements are level: teaspoons are assumed to be 5 ml, and tablespoons are assumed to be 15 ml.
- Unless otherwise stated, milk is assumed to be full fat, eggs and individual vegetables such as potatoes are medium, and pepper is freshly ground black pepper.
- Recipes using raw or very lightly cooked eggs should be avoided by infants, the elderly, pregnant women, convalescents, and anyone suffering from an illness.
- Optional ingredients, variations or serving suggestions have not been included in the calculations. The times given are an approximate guide only. Preparation times differ according to the techniques used by different people and the cooking times vary as a result of the type of oven used.

contents

introduction

Cooked in minutes and easy on the purse, pasta is one of the most versatile of foods, combining happily with a wide variety of sauces. Although meat-based sauces are among the best known, vegetables provide inspiration for many delicious sauces, as do fish and seafood.

Pasta comes in a large number of shapes: flat and round ribbons, tubes, quills and corkscrews, to name but a few. Each shape lends itself to a particular sauce style. For example, long, thin pasta, such as spaghetti, is best for tomato or oil-based sauces. The sauce coats the surface and clings to it as you twirl the pasta round a fork. Wide, flat ribbons, such as fettucine, go well with cream sauces. Shapes or short, hollow tubes are perfect for chunkier sauces because they trap tasty morsels in their crevices.

To cook perfect pasta, use a large pan so the pasta has enough room to move around freely. Allow 1 litre/1¾ pint water for every 115 g/4 oz pasta. Bring the water to a fast boil, then add the salt and pasta together, stirring once. Cooking time depends on the type of pasta. It is ready when al dente – tender, but still firm to the bite and slightly chewy. Be careful not to overcook. It is generally better to cook the sauce before the pasta; sauces can be kept waiting, but pasta cannot – it becomes sticky!

guide to recipe key		
	easy	Recipes are graded as follows: 1 pea = easy; 2 peas = very easy; 3 peas = extremely easy.
	serves 4	Recipes generally serve four people. Simply halve the ingredients to serve two, taking care not to mix imperial and metric measurements.
	10 minutes	Preparation time.
	10 minutes	Cooking time.

creamy chicken & shiitake sauce,
page 20

raw tomato sauce with olive oil,
garlic & basil, page 48

spaghetti with anchovies, olives, capers
& tomatoes, page 70

mussels with tomatoes,
peppers & olives, page 88

meat & poultry sauces

Rich, hearty, meat-based sauces include the universally popular spaghetti bolognese, which needs no introduction. There are also irresistible sauces made with coarse-cut sausages or bacon and enriched with tomatoes, mushrooms or peppers.
Less well-known are more delicate sauces made with chicken. These often include generous amounts of cream and freshly grated cheese for richness and flavour.
All the sauces are simple to prepare and are equally suitable for relaxed entertaining or family suppers.

classic bolognese
meat sauce

very easy	
serves 6 as a starter, 4 as a main course	
15 minutes	
1 hour 15 minutes	

ingredients

2 tbsp olive oil
1 tbsp butter
1 small onion, chopped finely
1 carrot, chopped finely
1 celery stick, chopped finely
50 g/1¾ oz mushrooms, diced
225 g/8 oz minced beef
75 g/2¾ oz unsmoked bacon
  or ham, diced
2 chicken livers, chopped

2 tbsp tomato purée
125 ml/4 fl oz dry white wine
salt and pepper
½ tsp freshly grated nutmeg
300 ml/10 fl oz chicken stock
125 ml/4 fl oz double cream
450 g/1 lb dried spaghetti
2 tbsp chopped fresh parsley,
  to garnish
freshly grated Parmesan, to serve

Heat the oil and butter in a large saucepan over a medium heat. Add the onion, carrot, celery and mushrooms to the pan, then fry until soft. Add the beef and bacon to the pan and fry until the beef is evenly browned.

Stir in the chicken livers and tomato purée and cook for 2–3 minutes. Pour in the wine and season with salt, pepper and the nutmeg. Add the stock. Bring to the boil, then cover and simmer gently over a low heat for 1 hour. Stir in the cream and simmer, uncovered, until reduced.

Cook the pasta in plenty of boiling salted water until al dente. Drain and transfer to a warm serving dish.

Pour half the sauce over the pasta. Toss well to mix. Spoon the remaining sauce over the top.

Garnish with the parsley and serve with Parmesan cheese.

macaroni with sausage, pepperoncini & olives

	ingredients	
very easy	1 tbsp olive oil	2 tsp dried oregano
	1 large onion, chopped finely	125 ml/4 fl oz chicken stock
serves 6 as a starter, 4 as a main course	2 garlic cloves, chopped very finely	or red wine
	450 g/1 lb pork sausage, peeled and	salt and pepper
	chopped coarsely	450 g/1 lb dried macaroni
10–15 minutes	3 canned pepperoncini, or other hot	12–15 black olives, pitted and
	red peppers, drained and sliced	quartered
	400 g/14 oz canned chopped	75 g/2¾ oz freshly grated cheese,
15 minutes	tomatoes	such as Cheddar or Gruyère

Heat the oil in a large frying pan over a medium heat. Add the onion and fry for 5 minutes until soft. Add the garlic and fry for a few seconds until just beginning to colour. Add the sausage and fry until evenly browned.

Stir in the pepperoncini, tomatoes, oregano and stock. Season with salt and pepper. Bring to the boil, then simmer over a medium heat for 10 minutes, stirring occasionally.

Cook the macaroni in plenty of boiling salted water until al dente. Drain and transfer to a warm serving dish.

Add the olives and half the cheese to the sauce, then stir until the cheese has melted.

Pour the sauce over the pasta. Toss well to mix. Sprinkle with the remaining cheese and serve at once.

meat sauce with mushrooms & tomatoes

		ingredients	
very easy		3 tbsp olive oil	4 tbsp tomato purée
		450 g/1 lb minced beef	2 tsp dried oregano
serves 6 as a starter, 4 as a main course		225 g/8 oz mushrooms, sliced thinly	salt and pepper
		4 spring onions, sliced thinly	125 ml/4 fl oz stock or water
		4 garlic cloves, chopped very finely	450 g/1 lb dried conchiglie or gnocchi
10–15 minutes		400 g/14 oz canned chopped tomatoes	freshly grated Parmesan, to serve
40 minutes			

Heat 1 tablespoon of the oil in a large frying pan over a medium heat. Add the beef and fry until lightly browned. Remove from the pan and set aside.

Add the rest of the oil to the pan and fry the mushrooms until softened. Stir in the onions and garlic, then fry for 2 minutes.

Tip the meat back into the pan and stir in the tomatoes, tomato purée, oregano, salt, pepper and stock. Bring the mixture to the boil, then reduce the heat and simmer over a medium–low heat for 30 minutes.

Cook the pasta in plenty of boiling salted water until al dente. Drain and transfer to a warm serving dish.

Pour the sauce over the pasta and toss well to mix. Serve with freshly grated Parmesan.

sausage & beef sauce
with peppers & tomatoes

very easy	
serves 6 as a starter, 4 as a main course	
15–20 minutes	
1 hour 15 minutes	

ingredients

2 tbsp olive oil
4 bacon rashers, chopped
1 onion, chopped finely
1 green pepper, seeded and
  chopped finely
50 g/1¾ oz mushrooms, sliced thinly
4 garlic cloves, sliced thinly
225 g/8 oz minced beef
225 g/8 oz coarse pork sausage,
  peeled and chopped

800 g/1 lb 12 oz canned
  chopped tomatoes
1 fresh bay leaf
6 tbsp tomato purée
4 tbsp red wine or stock
salt and pepper
450 g/1 lb dried penne or rigatoni
6 fresh basil leaves, shredded

freshly grated Parmesan, to serve

Heat the oil in a large frying pan over a medium heat. Add the bacon and fry until lightly browned. Add the onion, green pepper, mushrooms and garlic. Gently fry for 5–7 minutes until soft.

Stir in the beef and sausage, then cook until browned. Add the tomatoes and bay leaf. Bring to the boil, then simmer over a medium–low heat for 1 hour. Stir in the tomato purée and wine. Season with salt and pepper. Simmer for a few minutes more.

Cook the pasta in plenty of boiling salted water until al dente. Drain and transfer to a warm serving dish.

Pour the sauce over the pasta and toss well to mix. Sprinkle with the basil and serve with Parmesan.

chicken & onion
cream sauce

		ingredients	
very easy		1 tbsp olive oil	175 ml/6 fl oz milk
		2 tbsp butter	6 spring onions, green part included,
serves 4		1 garlic clove, chopped very finely	sliced diagonally
		4 boneless, skinless chicken breasts	35 g/1¼ oz freshly grated Parmesan
		salt and pepper	450 g/1 lb dried fettuccine
10 minutes		1 onion, chopped finely	
		1 chicken stock cube, crumbled	chopped fresh flat-leafed parsley,
		125 ml/4 fl oz water	to garnish
35 minutes		300 ml/10 fl oz double cream	

Heat the oil and butter with the garlic in a large frying pan over
a medium–low heat. Cook the garlic until just beginning to colour.
Add the chicken breasts and raise the heat to medium. Fry for
4–5 minutes on each side, until the juices are no longer pink.
Season with salt and pepper. Remove from the heat. Remove
the chicken breasts, leaving the oil in the pan. Slice the breasts
diagonally into thin strips and set aside.

Reheat the oil in the pan. Add the onion and gently fry for
5 minutes until soft. Add the crumbled stock cube and the water.
Bring to the boil, then simmer over a medium–low heat for
10 minutes. Stir in the cream, milk, spring onions and Parmesan.
Simmer until heated through and slightly thickened.

Cook the fettucine in boiling salted water until al dente.
Drain and transfer to a warm serving dish. Layer the chicken slices
over the pasta. Pour on the sauce, garnish with parsley and serve.

cannelloni with chicken, ricotta & herbs

		ingredients	
easy	MARINADE	1 tsp freshly ground black pepper
	125 ml/4 fl oz white wine vinegar	¼ tsp freshly grated nutmeg
	1 garlic clove, crushed	55 g/2 oz freshly grated Parmesan
serves 4	225 ml/8 fl oz olive oil	450 g/1 lb ricotta cheese
		1 egg, lightly beaten
15–20 minutes +30 minutes to marinate	2 tbsp olive oil	1 tbsp chopped fresh oregano
	4 boneless, skinless chicken breasts, diced	2 tbsp chopped fresh basil
		225 g/8 oz dried cannelloni
	6 tbsp butter	75 g/2¾ oz freshly grated mozzarella
1 hour	500 ml/18 fl oz double cream	
	1 tsp salt	

In a bowl, combine the vinegar, garlic and olive oil for the marinade. Add the chicken and marinate for 30 minutes.

Heat 2 tablespoons of olive oil in a frying pan. Drain the chicken and cook 5–7 minutes, stirring, until no longer pink. Set aside.

Melt the butter in a saucepan over a medium–high heat. Add the cream, salt, pepper and nutmeg. Stir until thickened. Reduce the heat, add the Parmesan and stir until melted. Remove from the heat.

Heat the oven to 180°C/350°F/Gas Mark 4. In a large bowl, mix together the ricotta, egg and herbs. Stir in the chicken. Stuff the cannelloni with the chicken mixture. Pour half the sauce into a 23 x 33 cm/9 x 13 inch baking dish. Place the stuffed cannelloni on top. Pour over the remaining sauce. Sprinkle with the mozzarella and cover with aluminium foil. Bake for 45 minutes. Leave the dish to stand for 10 minutes before serving.

creamy chicken
& shiitake sauce

		ingredients	
very easy		25 g/1 oz dried shiitake mushrooms	1 tsp fresh oregano or marjoram,
		350 ml/12 fl oz hot water	chopped finely
		1 tbsp olive oil	250 ml/9 fl oz chicken stock
serves 4		6 bacon rashers, chopped	300 ml/10 fl oz whipping cream
		3 boneless, skinless chicken breasts,	salt and pepper
10 minutes plus 30 minutes soaking time		sliced into strips	450 g/1 lb dried tagliatelle
		115 g/4 oz fresh shiitake	55 g/2 oz freshly grated Parmesan
		mushrooms, sliced	
		1 small onion, chopped finely	chopped fresh flat-leafed parsley,
35 minutes			to garnish

Put the dried mushrooms in a bowl with the hot water. Leave to soak for 30 minutes until softened. Remove, squeezing excess water back into the bowl. Strain the liquid in a fine-meshed sieve and reserve. Slice the soaked mushrooms, discarding the stems.

Heat the oil in a large frying pan over a medium heat. Add the bacon and chicken, then stir-fry for about 3 minutes. Add the dried and fresh mushrooms, the onion and oregano. Stir-fry for 5–7 minutes until soft. Pour in the stock and the mushroom liquid. Bring to the boil, stirring. Simmer briskly for about 10 minutes, continuing to stir, until reduced. Add the cream and simmer for 5 minutes, stirring, until beginning to thicken. Season with salt and pepper. Remove the pan from the heat and set aside.

Cook the pasta until al dente. Drain and transfer to a serving dish. Pour the sauce over the pasta. Add half the Parmesan and mix. Sprinkle with parsley and serve with the remaining Parmesan.

farfalle with chicken, broccoli & roasted red peppers

		ingredients	
very easy	4 tbsp olive oil	300 g/10½ oz dried farfalle or fusilli
	5 tbsp butter	175 g/6 oz bottled roasted red
serves 4	3 garlic cloves, chopped very finely	peppers, drained and diced
	450 g/1 lb boneless, skinless chicken	250 ml/9 fl oz chicken stock
	breasts, diced	
15 minutes	¼ tsp dried chilli flakes	freshly grated Parmesan, to serve
	salt and pepper	
	450 g/1 lb small broccoli florets	
15 minutes		

Bring a large pan of salted water to the boil. Meanwhile, heat the olive oil, butter and garlic in a large frying pan over a medium–low heat. Cook the garlic until just beginning to colour.

Add the diced chicken, raise the heat to medium and stir-fry for 4–5 minutes until the chicken is no longer pink. Add the chilli flakes and season with salt and pepper. Remove from the heat.

Plunge the broccoli into the boiling water and cook for 2 minutes until tender-crisp. Remove with a perforated spoon and set aside. Bring the water back to the boil. Add the pasta and cook until al dente. Drain and add to the chicken mixture in the pan. Add the broccoli and roasted peppers. Pour in the stock. Simmer briskly over a medium–high heat, stirring frequently, until most of the liquid has been absorbed.

Sprinkle with the Parmesan and serve.

chicken with basil & pine kernel pesto

		ingredients	
very easy		PESTO	2 tbsp freshly grated pecorino
		100 g/3½ oz shredded fresh basil	2 tbsp vegetable oil
serves 4		125 ml/4 fl oz extra-virgin olive oil	4 boneless, skinless chicken breasts
		3 tbsp pine kernels	350 g/12 oz dried fettuccine
		3 garlic cloves, crushed	freshly ground pepper to taste
		salt	
10 minutes		55 g/2 oz freshly grated Parmesan	sprig of fresh basil, to garnish
15 minutes			

To make the pesto, put the basil, olive oil, pine kernels, garlic and a generous pinch of salt in a food processor or blender. Purée the ingredients until smooth. Scrape the mixture into a bowl and stir in the cheeses.

Heat the vegetable oil in a frying pan over a medium heat. Fry the chicken breasts, turning once, for 8–10 minutes until the juices are no longer pink. Cut into small cubes.

Cook the pasta in plenty of boiling salted water until al dente. Drain and transfer to a warm serving dish. Add the chicken and pesto, then season with pepper. Toss well to mix.

Garnish with a sprig of basil and serve warm.

noodles with chicken
satay sauce

		ingredients	
	very easy	2 tbsp vegetable oil	225 g/8 oz dried vermicelli
		450 g/1 lb boneless, skinless	or spaghettini
		chicken breasts, cubed	125 g/4½ oz smooth peanut butter
	serves 4	1 red pepper, seeded and sliced	1 tsp grated fresh ginger root
		4 spring onions, green part included,	2 tbsp soy sauce
		sliced diagonally	125 ml/4 fl oz chicken stock
	10 minutes	pinch of salt	
	20 minutes		

Heat the oil in a large frying pan over a medium heat. Add the chicken and fry for 5–7 minutes until no longer pink. Add the pepper and spring onions. Fry for 3 minutes until just soft. Remove from the heat.

Cook the pasta in plenty of boiling salted water until al dente. Drain and return to the pan.

Put the peanut butter, ginger, soy sauce and chicken stock in a large saucepan. Simmer over a medium–low heat, stirring, until bubbling. Add the cooked vegetables, chicken and pasta to the peanut mixture. Toss gently until coated with the sauce.

Transfer to a warm serving dish and serve immediately.

fusilli with bacon, eggs & mushrooms

		ingredients	
very easy		1 tbsp olive oil	115 g/4 oz Cheddar or mozzarella
		4 rashers streaky bacon or pancetta	cheese, cubed
serves 6 as a starter, 4 as a main course		115 g/4 oz mushrooms, sliced	
		225 g/8 oz fusilli or conchiglie	chopped fresh flat-leafed parsley,
		salt and pepper	to garnish
		2 eggs, beaten	
10 minutes			
15 minutes			

Heat the oil in a frying pan over a medium heat. Add the bacon and fry until crisp. Remove with tongs, leaving the drippings in the pan. Cut into small pieces and keep warm.

Fry the mushrooms in the bacon drippings for 5–7 minutes until soft. Remove from the heat.

Cook the pasta in plenty of boiling salted water until al dente. Drain and return to the pan.

Stir the mushrooms, beaten eggs and the cheese cubes into the pasta. Season with pepper and toss until the eggs have coated the pasta and the cheese has melted.

Transfer to a warm serving dish. Sprinkle with the bacon pieces and parsley and serve at once.

rigatoni with spicy bacon & tomato sauce

		ingredients	
	very easy	6 tbsp olive oil	salt and pepper
		3 garlic cloves, sliced thinly	450 g/1 lb rigatoni
	serves 4	75 g/2¾ oz streaky bacon, chopped	10 fresh basil leaves, shredded
		800 g/1 lb 12 oz canned	2 tbsp freshly grated pecorino
		chopped tomatoes	
	10 minutes	½ tsp dried chilli flakes	
	45 minutes		

Heat the oil and garlic in a large frying pan over a medium–low heat. Cook until the garlic is just beginning to colour. Add the bacon and cook until browned.

Stir in the tomatoes and chilli flakes. Season with a little salt and pepper. Bring to the boil, then simmer over a medium–low heat for 30–40 minutes, until the oil separates from the tomatoes.

Cook the pasta in plenty of boiling salted water until al dente. Drain and transfer to a warm serving dish.

Pour the sauce over the pasta. Add the basil and pecorino, then toss well to mix. Serve at once.

ham, tomato & chilli sauce

		ingredients	
very easy	1 tbsp olive oil	800 g/1 lb 12 oz canned
	2 tbsp butter	chopped tomatoes
	1 onion, chopped finely	salt and pepper
serves 4	150 g/5½ oz ham, diced	450 g/1 lb bucatini or penne
	2 garlic cloves, chopped very finely	2 tbsp chopped fresh
	1 fresh red chilli, seeded and	flat-leafed parsley
10–15 minutes	chopped finely	6 tbsp freshly grated Parmesan
1 hour		

Put the olive oil and 1 tablespoon of the butter in a large saucepan over a medium–low heat. Add the onion and fry for 10 minutes until soft and golden. Add the ham and fry for 5 minutes until lightly browned. Stir in the garlic, chilli and tomatoes. Season with a little salt and pepper. Bring to the boil, then simmer over a medium–low heat for 30–40 minutes until thickened.

Cook the pasta in plenty of boiling salted water until al dente. Drain and transfer to a warm serving dish.

Pour the sauce over the pasta. Add the parsley, Parmesan and the remaining butter. Toss well to mix. Serve immediately.

spaghetti alla carbonara

		ingredients	
very easy	2 tbsp olive oil	20 g/¾ oz freshly grated pecorino
	1 tbsp butter	1 tbsp chopped fresh
serves 4	175 g/6 oz smoked streaky bacon,	flat-leafed parsley
	sliced into thin strips	4 tbsp single cream
	3 eggs, lightly beaten	pepper
10–15 minutes	35 g/1¼ oz freshly grated Parmesan	450 g/1 lb dried spaghetti
15 minutes		

Heat the oil and butter in a frying pan over a medium–high heat. Add the bacon and fry for 4–5 minutes until browned. Remove from the heat. Combine the eggs, cheeses, parsley and cream in a bowl, mixing well. Season with pepper.

Cook the pasta in plenty of boiling salted water until al dente. Drain and return to the pan.

Quickly add the egg mixture to the pasta, tossing rapidly so that the egg cooks in the heat. Transfer to a warm serving dish.

Briefly reheat the bacon over a high heat. Add to the pasta, toss again and serve at once.

vegetable sauces

With their flamboyant colours and fresh flavours, Mediterranean-style vegetables and herbs are perfect for pasta sauces. These are among the quickest and easiest sauces to prepare, ranging from the simple concoctions of chopped raw tomatoes, olive oil and basil to more complex mixtures of roasted peppers and garlic, or asparagus and Gorgonzola. Storecupboard ingredients are put to good use: jars of artichokes, peppers, sun-dried tomatoes and olives all contribute robust flavours that will please vegetarians and meat-eaters alike.

sun-dried tomato
& goat's cheese sauce

		ingredients	
very easy		1 tbsp butter	salt and pepper
		2 garlic cloves, sliced thinly	450 g/1 lb dried penne
		225 g/8 oz goat's cheese, crumbled	
serves 4		300 ml/10 fl oz milk	TO SERVE
		150 ml/5 fl oz double cream	35 g/1¼ oz freshly grated Parmesan
		20 oil-cured sun-dried tomato halves	10 fresh basil leaves, shredded
10 minutes		(in oil), chopped roughly	
10–15 minutes			

Heat the butter and garlic in a frying pan over a medium–low heat. Cook until the garlic is just beginning to colour. Add the cheese and milk. Stir until the cheese has melted and formed a thick sauce.

Add the cream and sun-dried tomatoes. Cook for about 5 minutes, stirring frequently, until reduced by one-third. Season with salt and pepper. Remove from the heat.

Cook the pasta in plenty of boiling salted water until al dente. Transfer to a warm serving dish.

Briefly reheat the sauce over low heat. Pour over the pasta. Add the Parmesan and basil, then toss well to mix. Serve immediately.

sun-dried tomato
sauce with herbs

very easy		
serves 4		
10–15 minutes		
20–25 minutes		

ingredients

85 g/3 oz sun-dried tomatoes
(not in oil)
700 ml/1¼ pints boiling water
2 tbsp olive oil
1 onion, chopped finely
2 large garlic cloves, sliced finely
2 tbsp chopped fresh
   flat-leafed parsley

2 tsp chopped fresh oregano
1 tsp chopped fresh rosemary
salt and pepper
350 g/12 oz dried fusilli

TO SERVE
10 fresh basil leaves, shredded
3 tbsp freshly grated Parmesan

Put the tomatoes and boiling water in a bowl and leave to stand for 5 minutes. Using a perforated spoon, remove one-third of the tomatoes from the bowl. Cut into bite-sized pieces. Put the remaining tomatoes and water into a blender and purée.

Heat the oil in a large frying pan over a medium heat. Add the onion and gently fry for 5 minutes until soft. Add the garlic and fry until just beginning to colour. Add the puréed tomato and the reserved tomato pieces to the pan. Bring to the boil, then simmer over a medium–low heat for 10 minutes. Stir in the herbs and season with salt and pepper. Simmer for 1 minute, then remove from the heat.

Cook the pasta in plenty of boiling salted water until al dente. Drain and transfer to a warm serving dish. Briefly reheat the sauce. Pour over the pasta, add the basil and toss well to mix. Sprinkle with the Parmesan and serve immediately.

tomato-chilli sauce
with avocado & coriander

		ingredients	
very easy		3 tbsp olive oil	salt and pepper
		4 spring onions, green part included, sliced finely	350 g/12 oz dried farfalle or conchiglie
serves 4		1 fresh green chilli, seeded and chopped very finely	2 small avocados, peeled and cubed
		2 garlic cloves, chopped very finely	juice of ½ lime
15 minutes		200 g/7 oz canned chopped tomatoes	6 tbsp chopped fresh coriander
20 minutes			

Heat 1 tablespoon of the oil in a frying pan over a medium–low heat. Add the spring onions and chilli, then fry, stirring constantly, for 3–4 minutes until just soft. Add the garlic and fry until just beginning to colour.

Stir in the tomatoes. Bring to the boil, then simmer the sauce over a medium heat for 10 minutes, stirring, until thickened. Season with salt and pepper.

Cook the pasta in plenty of boiling salted water until al dente. Drain and transfer to a warm serving dish.

Pour the sauce over the pasta. Add the avocados, lime juice, coriander and remaining olive oil. Toss well to mix. Serve warm or at room temperature.

pepper & goat's cheese sauce

		ingredients	
	very easy	2 tbsp olive oil	salt and pepper
		1 tbsp butter	450 g/1 lb dried rigatoni or penne
	serves 4	1 small onion, chopped finely	125 g/4½ oz goat's cheese, crumbled
		4 peppers, yellow and red, seeded	15 fresh basil leaves, shredded
		and cut into 2 cm/¾ inch squares	10 black olives, pitted and sliced
	10 minutes	3 garlic cloves, sliced thinly	
	30 minutes		

Heat the oil and butter in a large frying pan over a medium heat. Add the onion and fry until soft. Raise the heat to medium–high and add the peppers and garlic. Cook for 12–15 minutes, stirring, until the peppers are tender but not mushy. Season with salt and pepper. Remove from the heat.

Cook the pasta in plenty of boiling salted water until al dente. Drain and transfer to a warm serving dish. Add the goat's cheese and toss to mix.

Briefly reheat the sauce. Add the basil and olives. Pour over the pasta and toss well to mix. Serve immediately.

tomato sauce
with garlic & basil

		ingredients	
very easy		5 tbsp extra-virgin olive oil	450 g/1 lb dried spaghetti
		1 onion, chopped finely	large handful fresh basil leaves,
serves 4		800 g/1 lb 12 oz canned	shredded
		chopped tomatoes	
		4 garlic cloves, quartered	freshly grated Parmesan, to serve
10 minutes		salt and pepper	
30 minutes			

Heat the oil in a large saucepan over a medium heat. Add the onion and fry gently for 5 minutes until soft. Add the tomatoes and garlic. Bring to the boil, then simmer over a medium–low heat for 25–30 minutes until the oil separates from the tomato. Season with salt and pepper.

Cook the pasta in plenty of boiling salted water until al dente. Drain and transfer to a warm serving dish.

Pour the sauce over the pasta. Add the basil and toss well to mix. Serve with Parmesan.

raw tomato sauce with
olive oil, garlic & basil

		ingredients
extremely easy	550 g/1 lb 4 oz large, ripe tomatoes, peeled, deseeded and diced	3 tbsp chopped fresh oregano or marjoram
serves 4	125 ml/4 fl oz extra-virgin olive oil 4 garlic cloves, chopped very finely large handful fresh basil leaves, shredded	salt and pepper 450 g/1 lb dried conchiglie
10 minutes + 30 minutes standing time		
8–10 minutes		

Combine the tomatoes, olive oil, garlic, basil and oregano in a bowl that is large enough to eventually accommodate the cooked pasta. Season generously with salt and pepper. Cover the bowl with clingfilm and leave to stand at room temperature for at least 30 minutes.

Cook the pasta in plenty of boiling salted water until al dente. Drain thoroughly and immediately add to the tomatoes.

Toss well to mix. Serve at room temperature.

cherry tomato sauce
with olives

		ingredients	
very easy		4 tbsp olive oil	20–25 black olives, pitted and sliced
		900 g/2 lb cherry tomatoes	pepper
serves 4		2 garlic cloves, chopped very finely	350 g/12 oz dried conchiglie
		1 tbsp chopped fresh oregano	rind of ½ lemon, grated
		or marjoram	20 g/¾ oz freshly grated Parmesan
10 minutes		¼ tsp dried chilli flakes	
30 minutes			

Heat the oil in a large frying pan over a medium–high heat. Add the cherry tomatoes and stir until evenly coated with oil. Cover and cook for 10–12 minutes, shaking the pan and stirring once, until all the tomatoes have split.

Add the garlic, oregano, chilli flakes and olives. Season with pepper. Reduce the heat to low and simmer, uncovered, for another 7–10 minutes.

Cook the pasta in plenty of boiling salted water until al dente. Drain well and transfer to a warm serving dish.

Pour half the sauce over the pasta. Toss well to mix. Spoon the rest of the sauce over the top. Sprinkle with the grated lemon rind and Parmesan and serve at once.

roasted red pepper sauce

		ingredients
very easy	4 red peppers, halved and deseeded 5 tbsp olive oil	salt and pepper 350 g/12 oz dried penne or rigatoni
serves 4	1 small red onion, sliced finely 2 garlic cloves, chopped very finely 2 tbsp chopped fresh flat-leafed parsley	TO SERVE 4 tbsp toasted fresh breadcrumbs freshly grated Parmesan
10 minutes	1 tsp chopped fresh thyme	
35 minutes		

Place the peppers cut side down in a roasting tin. Roast in a preheated oven at 220°C/425°F/Gas Mark 7 for 15–20 minutes until the skin begins to blacken. Leave to cool slightly. Remove the skin from the peppers. Slice the flesh into thin strips.

Heat the oil in a large frying pan over a medium heat. Add the onion and fry for 5 minutes until soft. Add the garlic and fry until just beginning to colour. Stir in the roasted pepper strips, parsley and thyme. Season with salt and pepper. Stir until heated through.

Cook the pasta in plenty of boiling salted water until al dente. Drain well and transfer to a warm serving dish.

Pour the sauce over the pasta and toss well to mix. Sprinkle with the breadcrumbs and serve with Parmesan.

roasted garlic
& red pepper sauce

		ingredients	
	very easy	6 large garlic cloves, unpeeled	1 tsp chopped fresh thyme or oregano
		400 g/14 oz bottled roasted red	salt and pepper
	serves 4	peppers, drained and sliced	350 g/12 oz dried spaghetti, bucatini
		200 g/7 oz canned chopped tomatoes	or linguine
		3 tbsp olive oil	
	10 minutes	¼ tsp dried chilli flakes	freshly grated Parmesan, to serve
	30 minutes		

Place the unpeeled garlic cloves in a shallow, ovenproof dish. Roast in a preheated oven at 200°C/400°F/Gas Mark 6 for 7–10 minutes until the cloves feel soft.

Put the peppers, tomatoes and oil in a food processor or blender, then purée. Squeeze the garlic flesh into the purée. Add the chilli flakes and oregano. Season with salt and pepper. Blend again, then scrape into a saucepan and set aside.

Cook the pasta in plenty of boiling salted water until al dente. Drain and transfer to a warm serving dish.

Reheat the sauce and pour over the pasta. Toss well to mix. Serve at once with Parmesan.

marinated artichoke sauce
with onions & tomatoes

very easy	
serves 4	
10 minutes	
50 minutes	

ingredients

280 g/10 oz marinated artichoke
   hearts (in jar)
3 tbsp olive oil
1 onion, chopped finely
3 garlic cloves, chopped very finely
1 tsp dried oregano
¼ tsp dried chilli flakes

400 g/14 oz canned
   chopped tomatoes
salt and pepper
350 g/12 oz dried conchiglie
20 g/¾ oz freshly grated Parmesan
3 tbsp chopped fresh
   flat-leafed parsley

Drain the artichoke hearts, reserving the marinade. Heat the oil in a large saucepan over a medium heat. Add the onion and fry for 5 minutes until translucent. Add the garlic, oregano, chilli flakes and the reserved artichoke marinade. Cook for 5 more minutes.

Stir in the tomatoes. Bring to the boil, then simmer over a medium–low heat for 30 minutes. Season generously with salt and pepper.

Cook the pasta in plenty of boiling salted water until al dente. Drain and transfer to a warm serving dish.

Add the artichokes, Parmesan and parsley to the sauce. Cook for a few minutes until heated through.

Pour the sauce over the pasta. Toss well to mix. Serve at once.

asparagus & gorgonzola sauce with cream

		ingredients
	extremely easy	450 g/1 lb asparagus tips
		olive oil
	serves 4	salt and pepper
		225 g/8 oz Gorgonzola, crumbled
		175 ml/6 fl oz double cream
	10 minutes	350 g/12 oz dried penne
	20 minutes	

Place the asparagus tips in a single layer in a shallow ovenproof dish. Sprinkle with a little olive oil. Season with salt and pepper. Turn to coat in the oil and seasoning.

Roast in a preheated oven at 230°C/450°F/Gas Mark 8 for 10–12 minutes until slightly browned and just tender. Set aside and keep warm.

Combine the crumbled cheese with the cream in a bowl. Season with salt and pepper.

Cook the pasta in plenty of boiling salted water until al dente. Drain and transfer to a warm serving dish.

Immediately add the asparagus and the cheese mixture. Toss well until the cheese has melted and the pasta is coated with the sauce. Serve at once.

spaghetti with
garlic & oil sauce

		ingredients
extremely easy		450 g/1 lb dried spaghetti
		salt
serves 4		125 ml/4 fl oz extra-virgin olive oil
		4 garlic cloves, chopped very finely
		¼ tsp dried chilli flakes
10 minutes		3 tbsp chopped fresh flat-leafed parsley
25 minutes		

Cook the pasta in plenty of boiling salted water until al dente. Drain and transfer to a warm serving dish. Season with salt to taste and keep the dish warm.

Heat the oil in a small saucepan over a medium–low heat. Add the garlic and chilli flakes. Cook for 1–2 minutes until the garlic is just beginning to colour. Immediately pour the contents of the saucepan over the pasta. Toss thoroughly to mix.

Sprinkle with the parsley and toss again. Serve immediately.

roasted garlic cream sauce

		ingredients
easy		2 large heads garlic
		600 ml/1 pint double cream
serves 4		3 thin strips lemon peel
		salt and pepper
		350 g/12 oz dried fettuccine
		or tagliatelle
10 minutes		35 g/1¼ oz freshly grated Parmesan
20 minutes		2 tbsp chopped fresh
		flat-leafed parsley, to serve

Separate the garlic cloves, removing as much of the papery skin as possible, but leaving a thin layer intact. Place the cloves in a shallow ovenproof dish. Roast in a preheated oven at 200°C/400°F/ Gas Mark 6 for 7–10 minutes until the cloves feel soft.

When the garlic is cool enough to handle, remove the skin. Put the cloves in a small saucepan with the cream and lemon peel. Bring to the boil, then simmer gently over low heat for about 5 minutes until thickened. Push the sauce through a fine-meshed sieve, pressing with the back of a wooden spoon. Return to the saucepan. Season with salt and pepper and set aside.

Cook the pasta in plenty of boiling salted water until al dente. Drain and transfer to a warm serving dish. Stir the Parmesan into the sauce and reheat gently. Pour the sauce over the pasta and toss well to mix. Sprinkle with the parsley. Serve immediately.

mushroom & spinach
sauce with feta

		ingredients	
very easy		3 tbsp olive oil	450 g/1 lb dried rigatoni
		225 g/8 oz mushrooms, sliced	250 g/9 oz trimmed baby spinach,
serves 4		2 garlic cloves, chopped very finely	chopped roughly
		2 tbsp chopped fresh	250 ml/9 fl oz hot chicken stock
		flat-leafed parsley	55 g/2 oz feta cheese, crumbled
15 minutes		salt and pepper	1 tsp chopped fresh thyme
20 minutes			

Heat the oil in a large frying pan over a medium–high heat. Add the mushrooms and fry for 5 minutes until the moisture starts to evaporate. Add the garlic and parsley, then cook for a few seconds more. Season with salt and pepper. Remove the cooking pan from the heat.

Cook the pasta in plenty of boiling salted water until al dente. Drain and immediately return to the pan.

Add the spinach, hot stock and the mushrooms to the pasta. Toss well until the spinach has wilted. Transfer to a warm serving dish. Sprinkle with the feta and thyme and serve at once.

courgette sauce
with lemon & rosemary

		ingredients	
	very easy	6 tbsp olive oil	450 g/1 lb small courgettes, cut into
		1 small onion, sliced very thinly	4 cm x 5 mm/1½ x ¼ inch strips
	serves 4	2 garlic cloves, chopped very finely	finely grated peel of 1 lemon
		2 tbsp chopped fresh rosemary	salt and pepper
		1 tbsp chopped fresh	450 g/1 lb fusilli
		flat-leafed parsley	4 tbsp freshly grated Parmesan
	10 minutes		
	20 minutes		

Heat the olive oil in a large frying pan over a medium–low heat.
Add the onion and gently fry, stirring occasionally, for about
10 minutes until golden.

Raise the heat to medium–high. Add the garlic, rosemary and
parsley. Cook for a few seconds, stirring.

Add the courgettes and lemon peel. Cook for 5–7 minutes,
stirring occasionally, until the courgettes are just tender. Season
with salt and pepper. Remove from the heat.

Cook the pasta in plenty of boiling salted water until al dente.
Drain and transfer to a warm serving dish.

Briefly reheat the courgettes. Pour over the pasta and toss well
to mix. Sprinkle with the Parmesan and serve immediately.

fish &
seafood sauces

Fish and seafood are ideal candidates for pasta sauces, especially if you stock up with storecupboard basics such as bottled clams and cans of tuna and anchovies. These need only the briefest of cooking times, allowing you to get a meal on the table in minutes. Prawns are an all-time favourite with pasta and are very versatile. They can be combined with tomatoes, garlic and chilli for a robust Mediterranean sauce, or sizzled oriental-style with ginger and spices. Smoked salmon, mussels and scallops can form the basis of rich cream or tomato-based sauces that are ideal for entertaining.

spaghetti with anchovies, olives, capers & tomatoes

		ingredients	
very easy	6 tbsp olive oil 4 anchovy fillets, chopped 2 garlic cloves, chopped very finely 800 g/1 lb 12 oz canned chopped tomatoes 1 tsp dried oregano	¼ tsp dried chilli flakes salt and pepper 350 g/12 oz dried spaghetti 10–12 black olives, pitted and sliced 2 tbsp capers, drained	
serves 4			
10 minutes			
35–40 minutes			

Heat the oil with the anchovies in a large frying pan over a low heat. Stir until the anchovies dissolve. Add the garlic and cook for a few seconds until just beginning to colour. Add the tomatoes, oregano and chilli flakes, then season with salt and pepper. Bring to the boil, then simmer over a medium–low heat for 30 minutes until the oil begins to separate from the tomatoes.

Cook the pasta in plenty of boiling salted water until al dente. Drain and transfer to a warm serving dish.

Add the olives and capers to the sauce. Pour over the pasta and toss well to mix. Serve immediately.

clam & tomato sauce

		ingredients	
very easy		400 g/14 oz clams or scallops in brine (in jar)	3 tbsp chopped fresh flat-leafed parsley
serves 4		4 tbsp olive oil	½ tsp dried chilli flakes
		4 garlic cloves, chopped very finely	salt
10 minutes		800 g/1 lb 12 oz canned chopped tomatoes	450 g/1 lb dried riccioli or fusilli
35 minutes			

Drain the clams or scallops, reserving the liquid from the jar.

Heat the oil and garlic in a large saucepan over a low heat. Cook the garlic for a few seconds until just beginning to colour. Add the tomatoes, the reserved clam juice, parsley, chilli flakes and a little salt. Bring to the boil, then simmer over a medium–low heat for 30 minutes until the oil separates from the tomatoes.

Cook the pasta in plenty of boiling salted water until al dente. Drain and transfer to a warm serving dish.

Add the clams to the sauce, stirring until heated through. Pour the sauce over the pasta. Toss well to mix. Serve immediately.

prawn sauce with tomatoes, garlic & chilli

		ingredients	
✎	very easy	4 tbsp olive oil	salt and pepper
		5 garlic cloves, chopped very finely	450 g/1 lb dried linguine or spaghetti
🍴	serves 4	400 g/14 oz canned chopped tomatoes	350 g/12 oz raw peeled prawns
		1 fresh red chilli, seeded and chopped very finely	2 tbsp chopped fresh flat-leafed parsley, to garnish
🥣	10 minutes		
🕐	35 minutes		

Heat 2 tablespoons of the oil and the garlic in a saucepan over a medium–low heat. Cook the garlic until just beginning to colour. Add the tomatoes and chilli. Bring to the boil, then simmer over a medium–low heat for 30 minutes until the oil separates from the tomatoes. Season with salt and pepper.

Cook the pasta in plenty of boiling salted water until al dente. Drain and return to the pan.

Heat the remaining oil in a frying pan over a high heat. Add the prawns and stir-fry for 2 minutes until pink. Add the prawns to the tomato mixture. Stir in the parsley. Simmer over a low heat until bubbling.

Transfer the pasta to a warm serving dish. Pour the sauce over the pasta. Toss well to mix. Sprinkle over the chopped parsley to garnish and serve immediately.

clam & leek sauce

		ingredients
very easy		400 g/14 oz clams in brine (in jar) 1 bay leaf
		3 tbsp olive oil salt and pepper
serves 4		2 large leeks (white part only), sliced 350 g/12 oz dried spaghetti
		lengthwise and cut into thin or linguine
		5 cm/2 inch strips
10 minutes		2 garlic cloves, chopped very finely 3 tbsp chopped fresh
		4 tbsp dry white wine flat-leafed parsley, to garnish
15 minutes		

Drain the clams, reserving the liquid from the jar.

Heat the oil in a large frying pan over a medium–low heat.
Add the leeks and garlic, then fry gently for 3–4 minutes until the
leeks are tender-crisp. Stir in the wine and cook for 1–2 minutes
until evaporated. Add the bay leaf, clams and the reserved liquid.
Season with salt and pepper. Simmer for 5 minutes, then remove
from the heat.

Cook the pasta in plenty of boiling salted water until al dente.
Drain and transfer to a warm serving dish.

Briefly reheat the sauce and pour over the pasta. Add the parsley
and toss well to mix. Serve immediately.

prawn & garlic sauce
with cream

		ingredients	
very easy		3 tbsp olive oil	350 g/12 oz raw peeled prawns,
		3 tbsp butter	cut into 1 cm/½ inch pieces
serves 4		4 garlic cloves, chopped very finely	125 ml/4 fl oz double cream
		2 tbsp finely diced red pepper	salt and pepper
		2 tbsp tomato purée	
15 minutes		125 ml/4 fl oz dry white wine	3 tbsp chopped fresh
		450 g/1 lb tagliatelle or spaghetti	flat-leafed parsley, to garnish
15 minutes			

Heat the oil and butter in a saucepan over a medium–low heat.
Add the garlic and red pepper. Fry for a few seconds until the
garlic is just beginning to colour. Stir in the tomato purée and
wine. Cook for 10 minutes, stirring.

Cook the pasta in plenty of boiling salted water until al dente.
Drain and return to the pan.

Add the prawns to the sauce and raise the heat to medium–high.
Cook for 2 minutes, stirring, until the prawns turn pink. Reduce
the heat and stir in the cream. Cook for 1 minute, stirring
constantly, until thickened. Season with salt and pepper.

Transfer the pasta to a warm serving dish. Pour the sauce over the
pasta. Sprinkle with the parsley. Toss well to mix and serve at once.

spicy prawn sauce
with ginger

		ingredients	
very easy		4 tbsp passata (sieved tomatoes)	450 g/1 lb dried flat rice noodles
		300 ml/10 fl oz single cream	3 tbsp vegetable oil
serves 4		1½ tsp grated fresh ginger	3 garlic cloves, chopped very finely
		¼ tsp cayenne	450 g/1 lb raw peeled prawns
		1 tbsp lemon juice	2 tbsp chopped fresh coriander
10 minutes		1 tsp ground cumin	
		1 tsp salt	
		¼ tsp pepper	
10 minutes			

Combine the passata, cream, ginger, cayenne, lemon juice, cumin, salt and pepper in a small saucepan, mixing well. Cook the mixture over a medium heat, stirring, until bubbling. Remove from the heat.

Cook the noodles according to the packet instructions. Drain and transfer to a warm serving dish.

Heat the oil and garlic in a large frying pan over a medium–low heat. Cook until the garlic just begins to colour. Add the prawns and raise the heat to medium–high. Stir-fry for 2 minutes until the prawns are pink. Stir in the sauce and 1 tablespoon of the coriander. Cook for another minute.

Pour the prawn mixture over the noodles. Sprinkle with the remaining coriander and serve immediately.

prawn sauce with
lemon & herbs

		ingredients	
very easy	350 g/12 oz dried spaghettini or vermicelli	3 tbsp chopped fresh flat-leafed parsley	
serves 4	4 tbsp olive oil 4 tbsp butter 8 spring onions, green part included, sliced thinly	3 tbsp shredded fresh basil 1 tbsp chopped fresh marjoram or oregano 2 tsp chopped fresh thyme	
15–20 minutes	450 g/1 lb raw peeled prawns juice and finely grated peel of ½ lemon	250 ml/9 fl oz chicken stock salt and pepper	
10 minutes			

Cook the pasta in plenty of boiling salted water until al dente. Drain and return to the pan and cover to keep warm.

Heat the oil and butter in a large frying pan over a medium–high heat. Add the spring onions and prawns. Stir-fry for 2 minutes until the prawns turn pink. Reduce the heat to medium. Stir in the lemon juice and peel, herbs and chicken stock. Season with salt and pepper. Simmer until heated through.

Transfer the pasta to a warm serving dish. Pour the prawn mixture over the pasta and toss well to mix. Serve immediately.

scallops with porcini & cream sauce

		ingredients	
	very easy	25 g/1 oz dried porcini mushrooms	250 ml/9 fl oz double cream
		500 ml/18 fl oz hot water	salt and pepper
	serves 4	3 tbsp olive oil	350 g/12 oz dried fettuccine
		3 tbsp butter	or pappardelle
		350 g/12 oz scallops, sliced	
	10 minutes +20 minutes soaking time	2 garlic cloves, chopped very finely	2 tbsp chopped fresh
		2 tbsp lemon juice	flat-leafed parsley, to serve
	25 minutes		

Put the porcini and hot water in a bowl. Leave to soak for 20 minutes. Strain the mushrooms, reserving the soaking water, and chop roughly. Line a sieve with two pieces of kitchen paper and strain the mushroom water into a bowl.

Heat the oil and butter in a large frying pan over a medium heat. Add the scallops and cook for 2 minutes until just golden. Add the garlic and mushrooms, then stir-fry for another minute.

Stir in the lemon juice, cream and 125 ml/4 fl oz of the mushroom water. Bring to the boil, then simmer over a medium heat for 2–3 minutes, stirring constantly, until the liquid is reduced by half. Season with salt and pepper. Remove from the heat.

Cook the pasta in plenty of boiling salted water until al dente. Drain and transfer to a warm serving dish. Briefly reheat the sauce and pour over the pasta. Sprinkle with the parsley and toss well to mix. Serve immediately.

tuna with garlic,
lemon, capers & olives

		ingredients	
	extremely easy	350 g/12 oz dried conchiglie or gnocchi	2 tbsp lemon juice
			1 tbsp capers, drained
	serves 4	4 tbsp olive oil	10–12 black olives, pitted and sliced
		4 tbsp butter	
		3 large garlic cloves, sliced thinly	
		200 g/7 oz canned tuna, drained	2 tbsp chopped fresh
	10 minutes	and broken into chunks	flat-leafed parsley, to serve
	10 minutes		

Cook the pasta in plenty of boiling salted water until al dente. Drain and return to the pan.

Heat the olive oil and half the butter in a frying pan over a medium–low heat. Add the garlic and cook for a few seconds until just beginning to colour. Reduce the heat to low. Add the tuna, lemon juice, capers and olives. Stir gently until all the ingredients are heated through.

Transfer the pasta to a warm serving dish. Pour the tuna mixture over the pasta. Add the parsley and remaining butter. Toss well to mix. Serve immediately.

mussels with tomatoes, peppers & olives

		ingredients	
	very easy	3 litres/5¼ pints mussels	¼ tsp dried chilli flakes
		1 large onion, chopped finely	salt and pepper
	serves 4	250 ml/9 fl oz dry white wine	450 g/1 lb riccioli or fettucine
		3 tbsp olive oil	10–12 black olives, pitted and sliced
		3 garlic cloves, chopped very finely	
	20 minutes	2 yellow peppers, deseeded and diced	6 tbsp shredded fresh basil, to serve
		400 g/14 oz canned	
		chopped tomatoes	
	20 minutes		

Clean the mussels by scrubbing the shells and pulling out any beards that are attached. Rinse well and discard any with broken shells and any that do not close when tapped. Put the mussels in a large saucepan with the onion and white wine. Cover and cook over a medium heat for 3–4 minutes, shaking the pan, until the mussels open. Remove from the heat. Lift out the mussels with a perforated spoon, reserving the liquid. Discard any that remain closed. Remove the rest of the mussels from their shells.

Heat the olive oil and garlic in a frying pan over a medium–low heat. Cook until the garlic is just beginning to colour. Add the peppers, tomatoes, chilli flakes and 4 tablespoons of the mussel liquid. Bring to the boil, then simmer over a medium heat for 15 minutes until slightly reduced. Season with salt and pepper. Cook the pasta until al dente. Drain and transfer to a serving dish. Add the mussels and olives to the sauce; stir until heated. Pour onto the pasta. Add the basil and mix well. Serve at once.

mussels with white wine, garlic & parsley

		ingredients	
	very easy	3.5 litres/6 pints mussels, scrubbed	5 tbsp chopped fresh
		1 large onion, chopped	flat-leafed parsley
	serves 4	3 garlic cloves, chopped	1 tbsp chopped fresh rosemary
		very finely	4 tbsp butter
		500 ml/18 fl oz dry white wine	salt and pepper
	20 minutes	1 bay leaf	450 g/1 lb dried tagliatelle or other
		2 sprigs of fresh thyme	broad-ribboned pasta
	10 minutes		

Clean the mussels by scrubbing the shells and pulling out any beards that are attached. Rinse well, discarding any with broken shells or that remain open when tapped. Put the onion, garlic, white wine, herbs and 2 tablespoons of the butter in a saucepan. Bring to the boil, then reduce the heat. Add the mussels. Season to taste. Cover and cook over a medium heat for 3–4 minutes, shaking the pan, until the mussels open. Remove from the heat. Lift out the mussels with a perforated spoon, reserving the liquid. Discard any that remain closed. Remove most of the others from their shells, reserving a few in their shells to garnish.

Cook the pasta until al dente. Drain and put the pasta into bowls. Spoon the mussels over the pasta. Strain the mussel liquid and return to the pan. Add the remaining butter and heat until melted. Pour over the pasta, garnish with the mussels in their shells and serve immediately.

smoked salmon, soured cream & mustard sauce

		ingredients	
extremely easy	450 g/1 lb tagliatelle or conchiglie	225 g/8 oz smoked salmon,
	300 ml/10 fl oz soured cream	cut into bite-sized pieces
serves 4	2 tsp Dijon mustard	finely grated peel of ½ lemon
	4 large spring onions,	pepper
	sliced finely	2 tbsp chopped fresh chives
10 minutes		
10 minutes		

Cook the pasta in plenty of boiling salted water until al dente. Drain and return to the pan. Add the soured cream, mustard, spring onions, smoked salmon and lemon peel to the pasta. Stir over a low heat until heated through. Season with pepper.

Transfer to a serving dish. Sprinkle with the chives. Serve warm or at room temperature.

hot cajun seafood sauce

		ingredients	
very easy		500 ml/18 fl oz whipping cream	450 g/1 lb dried fusilli or tagliatelle
		8 spring onions, sliced thinly	40 g/1½ oz freshly grated Gruyère
serves 4		55 g/2 oz chopped fresh	20 g/¾ oz freshly grated Parmesan
		flat-leafed parsley	2 tbsp olive oil
		1 tbsp chopped fresh thyme	225 g/8 oz raw peeled prawns
15 minutes		½ tbsp freshly ground black pepper	225 g/8 oz scallops, sliced
		½–1 tsp dried chilli flakes	
		1 tsp salt	
20 minutes			1 tbsp shredded fresh basil, to serve

Heat the cream in a large saucepan over a medium heat, stirring constantly. When almost boiling, reduce the heat and add the spring onions, parsley, thyme, pepper, chilli flakes and salt. Simmer for 7–8 minutes, stirring, until thickened. Remove from the heat.

Cook the pasta in plenty of boiling salted water until al dente. Drain and return to the pan. Add the cream mixture and the cheeses to the pasta. Toss over a low heat until the cheeses have melted. Transfer to a warm serving dish.

Heat the oil in a large frying pan over a medium–high heat. Add the prawns and scallops. Stir-fry for 2–3 minutes until the prawns have just turned pink.

Pour the seafood over the pasta and toss well to mix. Sprinkle with the basil. Serve immediately.

index